Images of
Rugby

Images of Rugby

The Breedon Books
Publishing Company
Derby

First published in Great Britain by
The Breedon Books Publishing Company Limited
Breedon House, 44 Friar Gate, Derby, DE1 1DA.
1996

ISBN 1 85983 062 5

Printed and bound by Butler & Tanner Ltd., Selwood Printing Works, Caxton Road, Frome, Somerset.

Colour separations by Colour Services, Wigston, Leicester.

Jackets printed by Lawrence-Allen, Weston-super-Mare, Avon.

Contents

Acknowledgements

We would like to thank everyone who has contributed towards this work, particularly the following sources for their help in providing pictures and information: Rugby School archives department, Rugby Cement, Rugby Library, Robert Hendry, John F.Hughes and Dennis Keen.

Introduction

by Peter Aengenheister
Editor, *Rugby Advertiser*

FALLING in the eastern side of Warwickshire, one of the most attractive counties in England, Rugby, birthplace of the game, is in a unique position for communications. Amid gently rolling countryside the town nestles close to the M1 and M6 motorways and the A14 which is dual-carriaged for almost its entire length to the east coast at Ipswich.

The original site of Rugby is very old and was bounded by two of the best known old Roman roads, the Fosse Way and Watling Street, which meet at nearby High Cross. It is also close to the link of major canal systems, the Grand Union Canal and the Oxford Canal. The Avon which passes through Stratford passes through Rugby too.

Rugby started to develop in 1255 after it became a market town, and its livestock market is one of the things it is well-known for now. In 1567, local grocer Lawrence Sheriff founded the world famous Rugby School, where in 1823 William Webb Ellis 'picked up the ball and ran' and introduced the game of rugby which now gives endless pleasure to millions around the world.

Rugby's other famous sons include poet Rupert Brooke, Lewis Carroll and Thomas Hughes, who added to the school's fame through his work, *Tom Brown's Schooldays*, which was based on life at the school.

In the 19th century Rugby became a major railway centre and the town expanded. Many of the people in Rugby worked on the railway over the years and today the population of the borough exceeds 86,000. Despite the ravages of the Beeching cuts of the 1960s, the railway remains important today – there are daily European services taking travellers from Rugby to Paris and the soon-to-be-completed rail freight terminal at nearby Crick will ensure the future of trade and business links with the continent.

Other major employers in Rugby include the GEC group and Rugby Cement, although the town has a bustling business and industrial sector in Swift Valley, and the nearby Magna Park where several worldwide international companies have their European distribution centres.

A visitor to Rugby has plenty to see, but also in the surrounding villages there is more – at Dunchurch is the home of Guy Fawkes, and at close-by Ashby St Ledgers is the room where the Gunpowder Plot was hatched.

Not far away is Braunston, a picturesque canal centre, and Naseby, scene of the famous battle in 1645 – Warwick and Stratford upon Avon are a few miles west. In compiling this book, we have sought to cover, in very broad strokes, life, past and present in the area.

Some Rugby History

All manner of events and occasions stand out as milestones in the history of Rugby. This section features a number of them, ranging from a fire at Holy Trinity Church to the unearthing of some old hand grenades.

An interior view of the now-demolished Holy Trinity Church.

The Armorial Bearings of Rugby Borough Council were conferred by letters patent on March 15, 1976. They incorporate the Arms of the former borough, which were granted in 1932. The griffins' heads, rose gules, lions' gambs and date branches originate from the Arms of Lawrence Sheriff – a Rugby grocer in the time of Elizabeth I.

The gold bezant enclosing the rose gules is a reference to Lawrence Sheriff's business, while the thunderbolts at the top refer to the town's electrical industry, and the wheel, the mechanical industry.

On the actual Arms, the bear and ragged staff are from the Arms of the Warwickshire County Council.

The eight circles (bezants) on the green border each represent five parishes of the former rural district.

The Borough motto – Floreat Rugbeia Major – means 'May greater Rugby flourish'.

The Holy Trinity Church, Clifton Road, before a fire in 1980 led to its demolition.

Firefighters try to calm the blaze at the Holy Trinity Church, Clifton Road, in 1980.

The demolition of Overslade Housing Estate in 1989.

This and the following two photographs show just some of the scenes from May 1932 when huge floods wreaked havoc in the town. A staggering 1.9 inches of rain fell on Rugby.

Pictured here are the staff of the Oxford Street Laundry, Rugby, on a trip to Bournemouth in 1919. The owners of the laundry, with their three children, are seated just behind the driver's seat.

This cottage off Brownsover Lane is reputed to be the birthplace of Lawrence Sheriff in around 1515, founder of Rugby School.

Joseph Norman, 70, Crimean War veteran, who saved Walter Scott Collins, aged three from drowning at Brownsover, Rugby, in June 1905. He was awarded a Certificate of Thanks and a monetary gift from the Royal Humane Society.

The last man to be put into the stocks at Rugby. William Jarvis was found drunk in 1865, brought before the local magistrates and fined five shilling (25p). He was placed in the stocks for six hours.

Pupils of Wood Street Infants School take an afternoon rest on upturned benches in 1928.

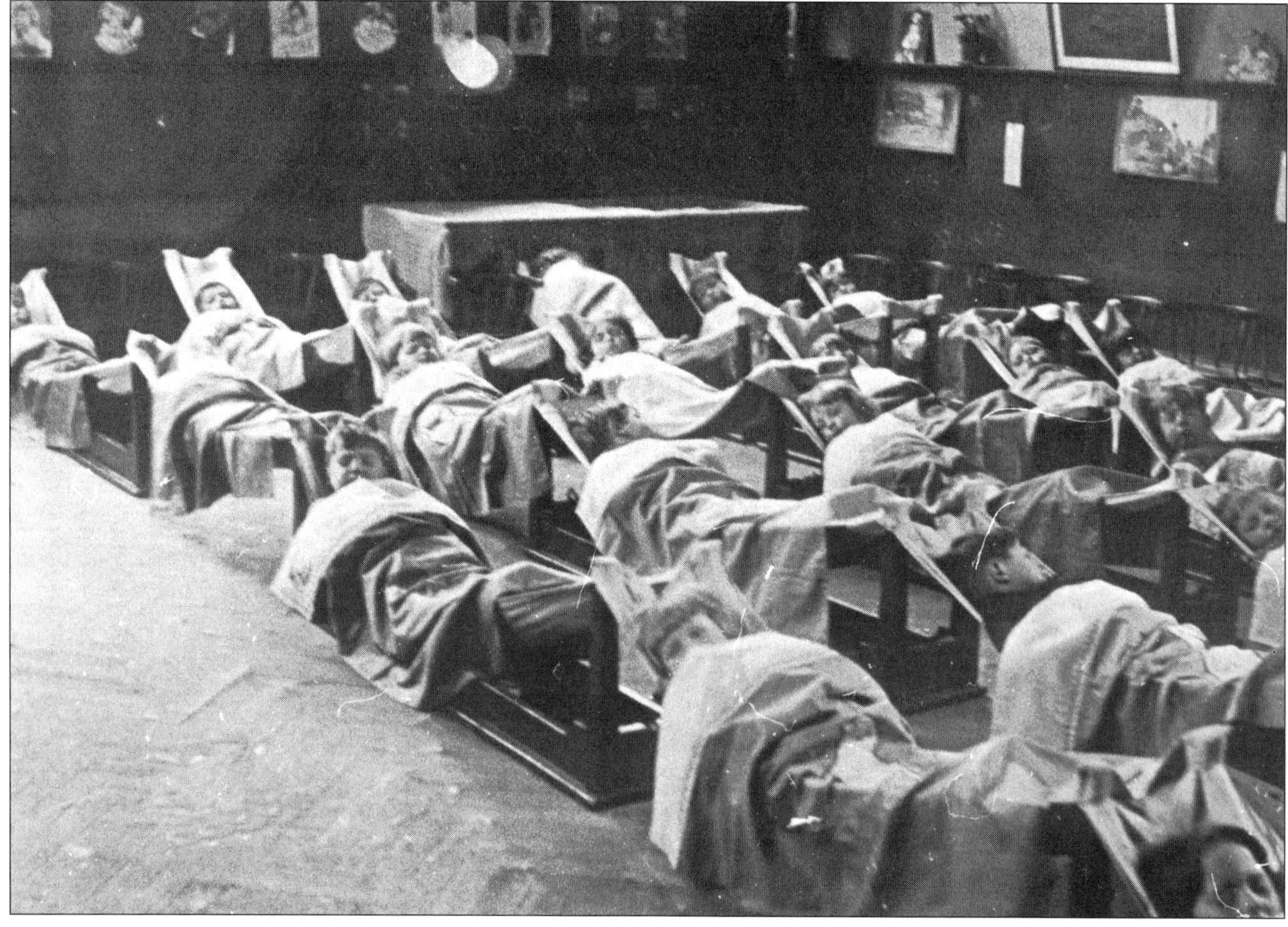

Corporal Barrie Brooks, Sapper Dave Starling and Corporal Mick Cursons examine old hand grenades they had unearthed.

Queues for taxis stretch all the way down North Street during the bus strike of December 1970.

An Evreux policeman steps in to direct Church Street traffic during a twin town visit in March 1970.

Rugby School

Rugby School has been at the heart of Rugby life for decades and in many respects it has been responsible for putting the town on the map. Many pupils have gone on to become national and international figures. The school buildings have also formed a landmark in the town and surrounding area.

An unusual view of Rugby School from the Northampton Road, drawn in 1861.

Rugby being played at Rugby School in 1832, from a painting by George Barnard.

Lewis Carroll took this photograph of boys at Rugby School in 1865.

Rugby School boys in Lawrence Sheriff Street returning for breakfast after early school.

Moving of the Great Elm just before the extension to Rugby School chapel in 1870. The tree survived the move but perished at the hands of Dutch Elm Disease this century.

The Temple Speech Room was decked out to herald the arrival of King Edward VII at Rugby School in 1909.

King Edward VII raises his top hat as he passes the Temple Speech Room during his visit to Rugby School in 1909.

King Edward VII smiles approvingly after planting a tree at Rugby School during his visit in July 1909.

Rupert Brooke's father, Parker Brooke (left) on The Close with the School Marshall in 1905.

Rupert Brooke, the poet, born in Rugby in 1887 and educated at Rugby School. He died during World War One, in 1915, two years after this picture was taken.

The Quadrangle at Rugby School.

The Close, Rugby School, where William Webb Ellis is reputed to have invented the game of rugby in 1823. The school chapel is in the background. This photograph was taken in 1938.

Field-Marshall Montgomery of Alamein on his first visit to Rugby School in 1947.

Rugby School pupils do a spot of log delivery through their social services scheme in 1970.

The Railways

Rugby is poised for a massive economic upturn following the launch of three direct trains a day to Paris and Brussels. These services, which will return later in the day, will also link up to trains serving Germany, Austria and Italy.

Talks are currently under way for a major facelift to Rugby railway station, described recently as the 'Gateway to Warwickshire'. The plans, being made by Rugby Partnership, will include a new entrance, car parking improvements, a new booking hall, brightening up of the station approach as well as a major revamp for the waiting room which is probably being redesigned as a departure point for European travellers.

Railway historians in the town believe that the introduction of the new direct link with Europe will restore the image and position of Rugby to that of the pre-1966 days when services were cut back as part of the Beeching plan.

At that time Rugby lost direct services to Peterborough, Leicester and Leamington Spa and there have been fewer inter-city services to other main towns and cities in the country.

Rugby is now expected to be the premier calling point for European passenger services with improved car parking facilities for travellers.

This and the following three pictures show versions of the main entrance to Rugby railway station. A further version is being planned, subject to a Government grant, shortly to be applied for as part of major modernisation works to various areas of the station. The oldest of the pictures shows an entrance now on the site of the present station approach.

RUGBY MIDLAND
IN
RUGBY MIDLAND

This 44-arm signal gantry at Rugby was the largest in the world. It was removed when electric colour light signalling was installed in October 1939.

These two views show the northern platform and southern platform respectively of Rugby station in the mid-1920s. There is a retail kiosk in the foreground, an idea which could be reintroduced following the planned improvements to the station, given approval of Government grant aid in 1996. The train approaching the platform is a local service to Brandon and Wolstan (a station long since demolished), Coventry and Birmingham.

Rugby railway's war memorial in the District Electrical Depot in Mill Road. A total of 20 employees from the steam sheds were killed during World War One and two others in World War Two. Below is the locomotive name plate Patriot, a travelling memorial to the Rugby men. This locomotive returned to Rugby every year until the 1960s. A service of remembrance is still held there annually.

This picture, was supplied by Bill Grace of Charles Street, Rugby, who is pictured without hat, with Fred Warwick. Both held the position of station foreman at Rugby. One of Mr Grace's proudest memories is the visit of Eleanor Roosevelt to the station in 1958 when the widow of former American president, Franklin D.Roosevelt, was touring Britain.

A shot of a steam-hauled southbound express running through Rugby signalbox opposite the old BTH works. The picture was taken from the wooden bridge.

A view of the wooden bridge, a main footway connecting the town with the BTH (now GEC) works, with an express travelling through.

Two of the largest signal boxes in Rugby before the advent of power signalling. Collectively they controlled the running of hundreds of passenger and freight trains.

The Duke of Edinburgh being escorted across Rugby station platform from the Royal Train in 1963. He was accompanied by the then Mayor of Rugby, Councillor Arthur Taylor. Behind, left, is the former Town Clerk of Rugby, Leo Duffy, and members of the Royal Household.

Rugby's new all-electric power box, opened in July 1964, replaces 22 manual old type signal boxes and controls about 90 miles of track. It covers from Brinklow on the Trent Valley line and Binley Colliery on the Coventry line to Roade in Northamptonshire. The console room is on the first floor and stores the main operating equipment. The console is 8ft high and 27ft long, showing all the routes under the control of the operators.

In the all-electric signalling system each train is identified to the signalman by the train identification code which is shown on the front of the locomotive and which is flashed on to an aperture at each signal in turn as the train moves along.

The Newcastle-Poole express, better known in Rugby as the Bournemouth Belle, arriving at Rugby Great Central station, now closed, at the start of Rugby's holiday fortnight. This was the last time that holidaymakers were able to use this train as the Central line south of Rugby closed in early September 1966. Thereafter only a local service between Rugby and Nottingham continued to operate.

One of the last remaining staff at work at Rugby's Great Central station was signalman Laurence Brewster. The picture was taken in February 1969 and the line closed as part of the Beeching cuts on 5 May that year.

British Rail's advanced passenger train photographed by *Rugby Advertiser* chief photographer John Albyn on its inaugural run to Euston. It passed through Hillmorton at a speed of 125mph and cut the travelling time to London by more than an hour. Its time for the 401-mile trip was 4hrs 13 mins. It clocked 137mph passing through Blisworth in South Northamptonshire.

One of the Anglo-Scottish crack locomotives running into Rugby on a journey to Euston.

The introduction of the Eurostar service to both Paris and Brussels in 1996 could substantially revitalise Rugby's economy. The shot in the arm provided by the new service, which will run three times a day from Rugby, will offer a direct link from Rugby to major European centres, in only a little over three hours travelling time via the Channel Tunnel. Eurostar can be distinguished from other high speed trains by its length and correspondingly higher seating capacity. With two power cars and 18 coaches it measures almost 400 metres and can accommodate 794 passengers.

From the prospect of Eurostar to an earlier time. A century after railway fever had first hit Rugby one enthusiast, the late Dr Robert Hendry, set up a full model train layout in his town centre house.

It occupies several bedrooms and an upstairs landing and both Dr Hendry and his son, Robert Powell Hendry, quickly became established authors of railway books.

Their interests in railways extended to the Isle of Man where, only a few years ago, a locomotive was named after the doctor.

The first photograph shows the late Dr Hendry with just some of the railway memorabilia which is still on the walls of the house. The second picture shows part of the massive rail layout.

The Streets of Rugby

Over the years the streets of Rugby have reflected the life of the town and this chapter is dedicated to all sorts of street life. The photograph features such a wide variety of subjects as royal celebrations and thriving back street business.

Back in the 1890s, numbers 14 and 15 Cross Street, Rugby, were a thriving game bird business. Today they are private houses.

This is West Street, Rugby, in about 1955. It was demolished to create a link road between Bilton Road and Newbold Road and was opened in May 1958, as Corporation Street.

Corporation Street which was developed in the 1950s.

These cottages are in North Street, where the NatWest Bank now stands.

This cottage was one of a pair, demolished a year after this photograph was taken in 1903. It made way for Park Road at the bottom of North Street.

This photograph of North Street was taken about 1895.

The Rugby Club in North Street is decked out with flags and shields to celebrate the visit of King Edward VII in 1909.

Benfield House was destroyed in 1930 to make way for the North Street Post Office. It was built in 1669 and stood in extensive grounds.

A view of North Street in the 1920s.

Another view of the cottages in North Street, near to where the entrance to the Clock Tower shopping precinct now stands.

This picture of North Street was taken from Market Place, with the Rugby Tavern, previously The Windmill on the left.

This picture of the junction of North Street with Park Road has a Barker & Dobson van making a delivery of confectionery.

This photograph of North Street was taken in the early 1950s. On the left can just be seen the NatWest Bank.

The lads were out in Market Place when this picture was taken some time after 1888 when the Clock Tower was built.

The last old house to be knocked down in North Street was also a barber's. Over the shop window was the name Foxon.

Rugby Market Place around 1890.

You don't see many of these in Market Place today. This charming picture was taken in 1895. Obviously the ladies knew how to dress for market day!

The Clock Tower around the turn of the century as the town pays respect to Queen Victoria in 1901. The cabin was used to shelter cabbies from the elements.

The date is November 15, 1938 and the Clock Tower is being used for advertising for volunteers for the emergency services as war clouds gather over Europe.

The Clock Tower and North Street pictured from St Andrew's Parish Church around 1930. There is just one car,

parked close to what is now the Rugby Tavern, and the horses and carriages were the only taxis available.

The busy Market Place in the early 1950s.

The Clock Tower is illuminated for the coronation of Queen Elizabeth II in June 1953.

A traditional English bobby directs traffic in Market Place in the mid 1950s.

Long before pedestrianisation and the Rugby Centre. This photograph was probably taken in the early 1970s.

This is the Methodist Church which stood in Market Place. The photograph was taken around 1980, after which the church was demolished and a replacement built in Russelsheim Way.

Enforced changes – one of the older houses in Warwick Street which was destroyed by fire in May 1905.

A view from St Matthew's Church, above Warwick Street, showing the cluster of Victorian houses.

The Star stood on Warwick Street, which is now part of the gyratory system. The pub was demolished and the site remains an open space.

An early picture of Lawrence Sheriff Street. In the house on the west corner of Sheep Street, kept by Dr Bloxham, lodged boys from Rugby School.

This is the same Lawrence Sheriff Street, many years later in the 1980s, showing the Merry Minstrel pub which still occupies the site today.

Sheep Street is one of Rugby's main shopping areas and one which has changed a great deal over the years.

Looking up Sheep Street towards Lawrence Sheriff Street in 1904.

This view of Sheep Street, looking back on the town centre, shows St Andrew's Parish Church before the second tower was built.

A view of Castle Street looking towards the town centre.

Castle Street, again shown before pedestrianisation.

High Street is right at the heart of Rugby town centre and has seen great changes over the years. It has been the scene of numerous civic activities as the Town Hall was originally housed there, in what is today

Marks & Spencer. This sketch shows a view of High Street in 1843, with the building on the right, now Briggs shoe shop, having changed very little.

High Street around the turn of the century.

High Street was packed on October 26, 1907 when HRH Princess Henry of Battenberg visited Rugby to open a new hospital children's wing. The princess was welcomed at the council chambers – the Benn Building, where Marks & Spencer's store now stands.

These two photographs show flags out in High Street to welcome King Edward VII when he visited Rugby on July 3, 1909.

A view of High Street, Sheep Street and Market Place in the 1950s.

This corner of High Street shows the Wine Barrel public house around 1980, where MacDonalds restaurant now stands.

Regent Street at the end of the last century.

Regent Street, with St Andrew's Parish Church in the background, in the first half of this century.

Women queuing for a sale at Yates clothes store, Regent Street, during World War Two.

Looking down from Regent Street at Regent Place, showing the Baptist Church and the public baths, where the statue of Rupert Brooke now stands.

A view inside the public baths on Regent Street in 1967.

This butcher's shop and shoemakers were situated in Church Street in 1860. The butcher's was run by Mr W.Lucas, who died in Kilsby in 1879.

The Grazier's Arms, Church Street, was one of the many pubs in Rugby where locals would drink and socialise in 1875, when this photograph was taken.

Not much of this scene remains today in Church Street, but The Squirrel pub is still there. The view was taken from the top of Holy Trinity Church tower in 1880. It shows most of the Gas Triangle, formerly known as the Horsepool End.

In 1887 the Golden Jubilee of Queen Victoria sparked these patriotic decorations in Church Street. One of them states: 'Our Queen For Fifty Years, God Bless Her.'

Lawrence Sheriff almshouses, Church Street, around 1900. The first four of these were built in 1567, for four old men, two from Rugby and two from Brownsover. Four more were added in 1783 and four more in 1828. They were demolished to make way for a parade of shops in 1961, and the new almshouses were built in Dunchurch Road.

Another view of the Lawrence Sheriff almshouses in Church Street.

One of the tenants of the Lawrence Sheriff almshouses in Church Street poses in his doorway in 1938.

The Pleasance in Church Street was the scene of serious shopping on Saturday mornings. This picture was taken

in 1980.

Gas Street car park, which became Rugby Market.

Rugby's General Post Office was opened in Albert Street in February 1901, in what was formerly a private house. In 1934 it moved to North Street and now, ironically, is back where it started. On the left of the doorway is Quigley's club.

These two 18th-century cottages in Pinders Lane, leading downhill from Castle Street, Rugby, survived until the 1930s.

Lawford Lane was decorated in 1897 to mark Queen Victoria's 60 years on the throne.

Clifton Road, showing Holy Trinity Church, which was closed and later knocked down. There is now a block of retirement homes on the site.

This was the scene at the junction of Whitehall Road and Clifton Road, Rugby, in the middle of the last century. It was known as The Old Whitehall.

A view of Clifton Road from further out of town, showing the large, impressive properties many of which still stand today.

The John Barford multi-storey car park going up in James Street in January 1990.

The John Barford car park in James Street under construction in February 1990.

The multi-storey car park nearing completion in October 1990.

Then and Now

One of the few parts of Rugby to retain an air of calm is Caldecott Park (sometimes spelt Caldicott) but there have been changes even here and the present entrance (*below*) is to the right of the original.

In 1989 the above was the scene in Overslade, Rugby, when the site was demolished to make way for Garyth Williams Close (*below*).

Newbold Quarry, off Parkfield Road, was transformed from a workaday site (*above*) to a beauty spot (*below*).

The thatched cottages pictured above no longer stand on the Lilbourne Road coming out of Clifton (*below*).

The Merry Minstrel pub now stands on the corner of Drury Lane and Lawrence Sheriff Street, Rugby (*below*). The picture above shows what appears to be a pub, too, and next to it is a lodging house for Rugby School boys. It was owned by Dr Bloxham.

The bottom of School Street, Hillmorton, has changed beyond recognition from the turn of the century (*above*) to today (*below*).

The original Avon Mill in Newbold Road (*above*) was run until 1872 by the Bagshaw family but it ran into financial problems, which may be why it was converted into a pub as well. The mills closed in 1930 but the pub (*below*) still flourishes.

Butler's Leap industrial area was so named because a Rugby School pupil named Butler apparently performed an amazing leap across the river. The bridge makes it easier these days (*below*) but the view has changed. Rugby golf course is to the right of the bottom picture.

Looking south down High Street, Rugby, around 1890 (*above*) shows little traffic. Today, there is less as the area is pedestrianised (*below*).

Warwick Street, Rugby, has not changed too much over the years, except that it has become part of the gyratory system since the picture (*above*) was taken in about 1930. St Matthew's Church still stands on the left (*below*) and the School, of course, still forms a fine skyline.

The name of Market Place is the only relic of the stalls that once stood regularly on the site. The picture (*above*) was taken around 1896 – eight years after the Clock Tower was built to commemorate Queen Victoria's Golden Jubilee. The market is now at the bottom of Castle Street and Gas Street.

Ladies in flowing skirts and beautiful hats grace Market Place in this photograph of Victorian Rugby (*above*). The building on the right between the two ornate street lamps is now the Alliance and Leicester Building Society (*right*).

LENNON
BROS Ltd
WHOLESALE
TOBACCO
Buckingham
NEXT
NEXT

The building on the fork of Sheep Street and High Street has hardly changed. But in 1897 it was Durrant's piano shop (*above*). Today it is Peter Briggs shoes (*below*). The early photograph also shows decorations marking Queen Victoria's Diamond Jubilee.

The Midland Bank appeared in Church Street in 1966 (*above*). Other than that the scene has not changed too much (*below*).

The George Hotel, which stood in Market Place, was demolished in 1846 and a new one built in its place (*above*). It closed in 1951 and was itself demolished two years later to make way for shops. H.Samuel's jewellers now stands on the site and the Clock Tower is the focal point of the area (*below*).

Quaint thatched cottages were once part of North Street (*above*). Today the NatWest Bank stands on the site and the street also houses an entrance to the Clock Tower shopping centre (*below*).

Money has changed hands on this North Street site for many years. The picture (*above*) shows it as the Post Office, where Barclays Bank stands today (*below*).

The Plaza Cinema at the bottom of North Street opened on January 30, 1933 (*above*). Thirteen years later it became the Grenada and in the early 1970s it closed and became a bingo hall which still operates (*below*).

The hunt posed for pictures in Dunchurch on this New Year's Day at the turn of the century (*above*). These days cars are parked on the same spot outside the Dun Cow (*below*).

The early 1960s seems the most likely date for this view (*above*) of Warwick Street, which is now part of the pass under the gyratory system (*below*).

Bequeathed to the town of Rugby in 1895 by Mr C.G.Benn, for use as the Town Hall, the Benn Buildings *(left)* are in the middle of the High Street. The building functioned as the Town Hall until 1936, when Marks & Spencer took over (*below*). The municipal offices were moved to large Victorian buildings in Newbold Road, before the current Town Hall was built on the Lawn Estates in 1961.

This is Sheep Street (*above*) before 1865 when the Hen and Chickens Inn, the two-storey building on the left, was demolished. Warwick House, next door, was demolished in 1959 and rebuilt. Today, trees give the street a softer image (*below*).

HILTONS
Boots
& Shoes
BOOTS HILTONS SHOES

Regent Street (*above and left*) is one of the least changed town centre areas in Rugby.

In contrast, the scene in James Street, Rugby, has changed in many respects, but the Alexandra Arms remains. New housing (*below*) replaces the older terraced homes (*above*).

You don't find many cattle wandering along Clifton Road (*above*) these days. Cars are more the norm today, as can be seen from the picture (*bottom*).

Rugby from the Air

Aerial views of the district give a completely different dimension to the local scene and this chapter gives a reflection of that.

Our first aerial view of Rugby is from 1988 and shows the town centre with Railway Terrace on the left and the James Street development on the right.

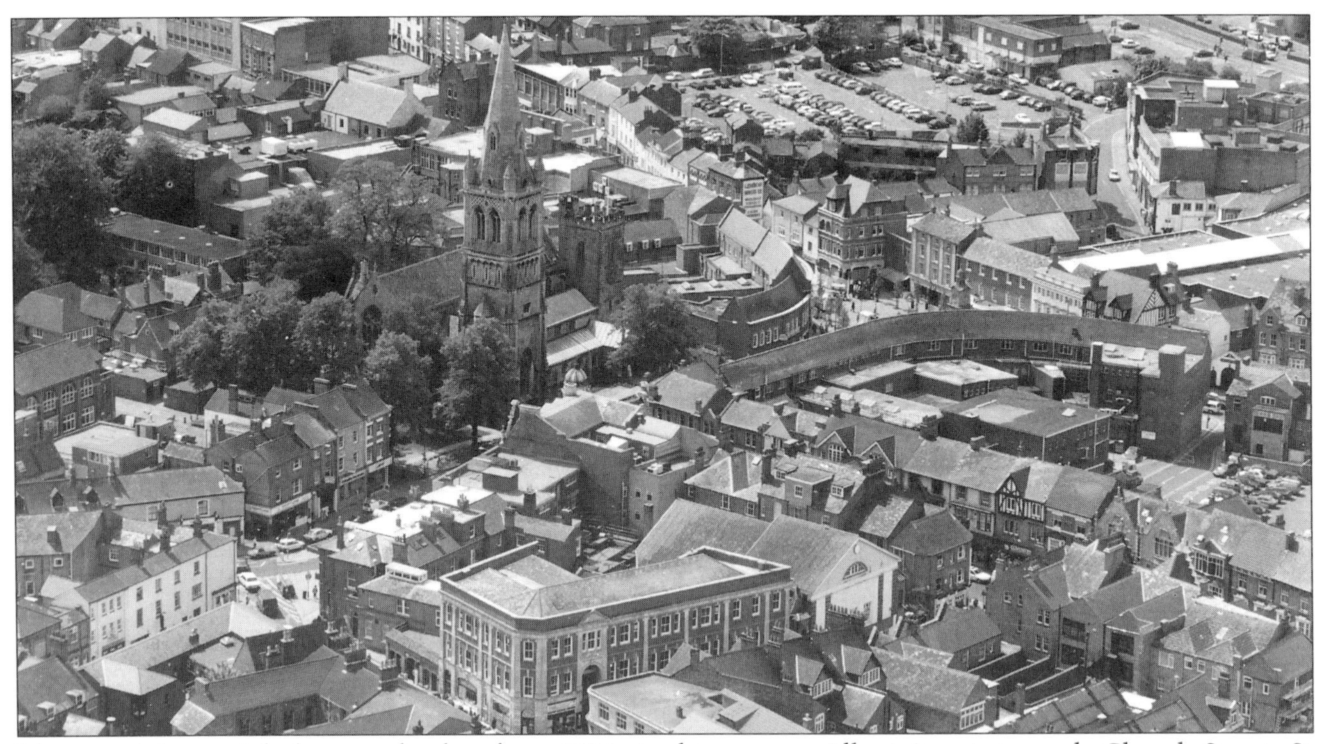

The remaining aerial photographs date from 1996. Looking across Albert Street, towards Church Street, St Andrew's Church and Market Place. The Chapel Street area of the town centre, which is due for re-development, can be seen in the background.

A view of Hillmorton with Watts Lane in the background and Hillmorton Middle School in the foreground

A view of Rugby Market on market day, looking up Castle Street and Church Street. The John Barford multi-storey car park is on the right in the foreground.

St Andrew's Church viewed from above the Clock Tower shopping precinct. North Street is in the foreground.

No failing to recognise a feature that dominates the Rugby skyline – the chimney and buildings of Rugby Cement works near Newbold.

Now saved, and with a new accident and emergency unit, is the Hospital of St Cross, Rugby with Barby Lane on the left-hand side.

Rugby School with The Close, cricket nets and the Rugby School chapel in the foreground.

A view along Clifton Road, with the tower blocks of Biart Place in the middle distance.

Clifton upon Dunsmore with the parish church in the foreground.

Boughton Road runs left to right with Howkins Road, Houston Road and Douglas Road running up to Reservoir Road across the top corner of the picture.

Gainsborough Crescent, with Constable Road running from the left to top right of the picture. Lower Street with the junction of School Street is on the bottom right-hand corner of the picture.

Royal Visits

Rugby has had its fair share of royal visits over the years – mostly to Rugby School and the Hospital of St Cross. Here are just a few of those visits recalled.

Flags were out for the visit of Princess Henry of Battenberg when she opened the children's wing of the Hospital of St Cross in 1907.

THE KING

Rugby and District Master Butchers' Association donated this ox in aid of the hospital when HRH the Duchess of York paid a visit in 1929.

The presentation of the standard to Rugby No 2 branch of the British Legion in April 1929 by HRH the Duchess of York, later Queen Elizabeth and now the Queen Mother.

HRH Mary, the Princess Royal, officially opened the Sun Pavilion at the Hospital of St Cross in October 1932. It was intended for the treatment of TB patients.

The heavens opened and so did the gates of Rugby School as Her Majesty the Queen, accompanied by HRH the Duke of Edinburgh, visited Rugby School in 1967 to officially name the Queen Elizabeth Gates in Barby Road.

A tree planted by the Queen commemorates her official visit to Rugby School in 1967.

In 1988 Princess Diana, patron of the Marriage Guidance Council (now Relate) visited the headquarters, Herbert Gray College in Little Church Street.

Princess Diana comes to Rugby in 1993 and meets Mayor Alan Webb (second right) and Red Cross officials.

In 1993, Princess Diana was greeted by scores of royal watchers when she visited Bosnian refugees at Fawsley House, Hillmorton Road, Rugby.

Princess Diana meets children from Bosnia at Fawsley House, Hillmorton Road, Rugby.

Famous Rugby People

Like most town's, Rugby has had its fair share of famous people who were either born in the town or have made their names there. This chapter highlights a few of them.

Sir Frank Whittle inventor of the jet engine, who had very strong Rugby area connections.

Rugby's MP since 1979 Jim Pawsey, pictured here with his wife Cynthia who was a leading light in the campaign to fund a Macmillan Nurse for Rugby.

Athlete Judy Livermore pictured on her return from the Moscow Olympics in 1980.

Memories of the great day in the town's footballing history, when VS Rugby won the FA Vase at Wembley in 1983, beating Halesowen Town 1-0. Here, manager Jimmy Knox celebrates with Barry Ferguson.

Above: Dave Ingram displays the FA Vase to jubilant Rugby supporters. Ingram returned to Butlin Road in 1993 as a member of the consortium which saved VS Rugby from extinction, after the club went into voluntary liquidation.

Far left: TV personality Peter Purves, who lived in Bilton for several years. He made his name as a presenter for the *Blue Peter* children's programme.

Left: Arthur Bostrom, star of BBC TV's *'Allo 'Allo* comedy programme and a former pupil at Lawrence Sheriff School.

Steve Hallard has been Britain's top archer for the last 15 years. He won Olympic bronze medals in 1988 and 1992 and is pictured here on his return from the Barcelona Games.

Sprinter Katharine Merry was the fastest 14-year-old the world had ever seen. She became European Junior 200 metres champion in 1993 and was the UK champion at both 100 metres and 200 metres. Katharine was pictured here in 1992.

Healing the Sick

Hospitals are at the heart of any community and Rugby is no different. This chapter shows the changes in the image of hospitals.

Wooden floors gleamed in Hatton Ward at Rugby's Hospital of St Cross at the end of the 19th century.

Music played a large part in the ceremony to mark the laying of the foundation stone of the children's ward at the Hospital of St Cross in 1907.

Young patients enjoy the facilities of the Sun Pavilion at the Hospital of St Cross.

The Lord Mayor of London laying a foundation stone of the new nurses' home at the Hospital of St Cross in May 1934.

A 1960s picture of the old accident and outpatient department at the Hospital of St Cross.

Can I help you? Switchboard operators at the Hospital of St Cross in 1990.

Builders make a start on the maternity block at the Hospital of St Cross.

Building work underway on the newer parts of the Hospital of St Cross.

Two views of St Luke's Hospital, Lower Hillmorton Road, which was demolished in the early 1990s. A modern housing estate and the Orchard Health Centre now stand in its place.

Rugby at Work

There has always been a variety of employment in Rugby and this chapter features photographs of some of the major companies which have provided jobs for the community. Some are large firms, some are not, but each has contributed tremendously to the life of the town and district.

A team of Rugby firefighters before the invention of the engine around the turn of the century.

Women busily making the balls for Gilbert's rugby football shop.

Baker and confectioner's shop on the corner of Arnold Street, Rugby.

Chalk being taken to the crushing plant by horse and cart at Rugby Cement.

Young employees at Rugby Cement at the turn of the century.

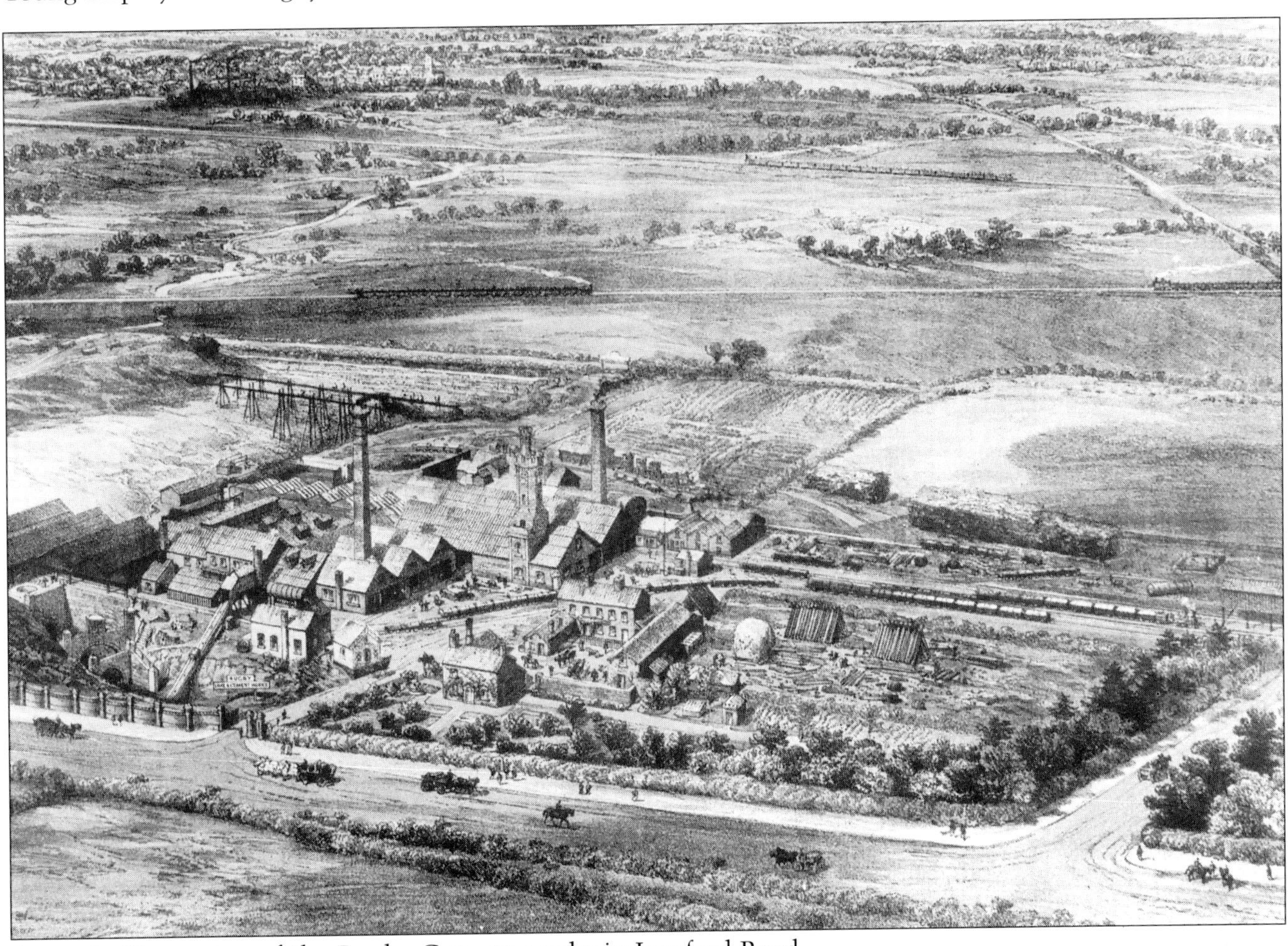

An early illustration of the Rugby Cement works in Lawford Road.

In 1966 two chimneys still formed landmarks at Rugby Cement works. Now there is one.

Rugby Cement works as it looks today.

The AEI works pictured in September 1925.

Members of the BTH Ex-Service Association. In the years after World War One such associations flourished all over

the country.

A service at the Mill Road war memorial.

Fun and games at the BTH Rag Day in 1934.

A band of Manchester United faithful supporters, who all worked in the Manchester construction office of BTH and are pictured after their team's promotion to the old First Division in 1936. Most of those pictured later moved to the head office in Rugby.

The voluntary fire brigade at GEC Willans works in 1937.

The BTH munitions factory at Mill Road, where electric torpedoes were manufactured.

Three bombs which fell on the Willans works in autumn 1941 broke windows and left two holes in the front of the building. A lone German bomber struck one Sunday afternoon and a member of the Home Guard, Alan West, returned fire with a single .303 shot, which earned him the nickname of 'Trigger'.

An aerial view of the GEC factories, with Brownsover estate in the background and Leicester Road on the left, taken in 1985 before the Tesco and Elliot's Field development.

The Alsthom's chimney disappears in a cloud of dust.

The demolition of GEC's Alsthom's chimney in June 1991. The Large Machines' 60-metre high chimney had dominated the skyline from Boughton Road for more than 80 years.

A view through the GEC works.

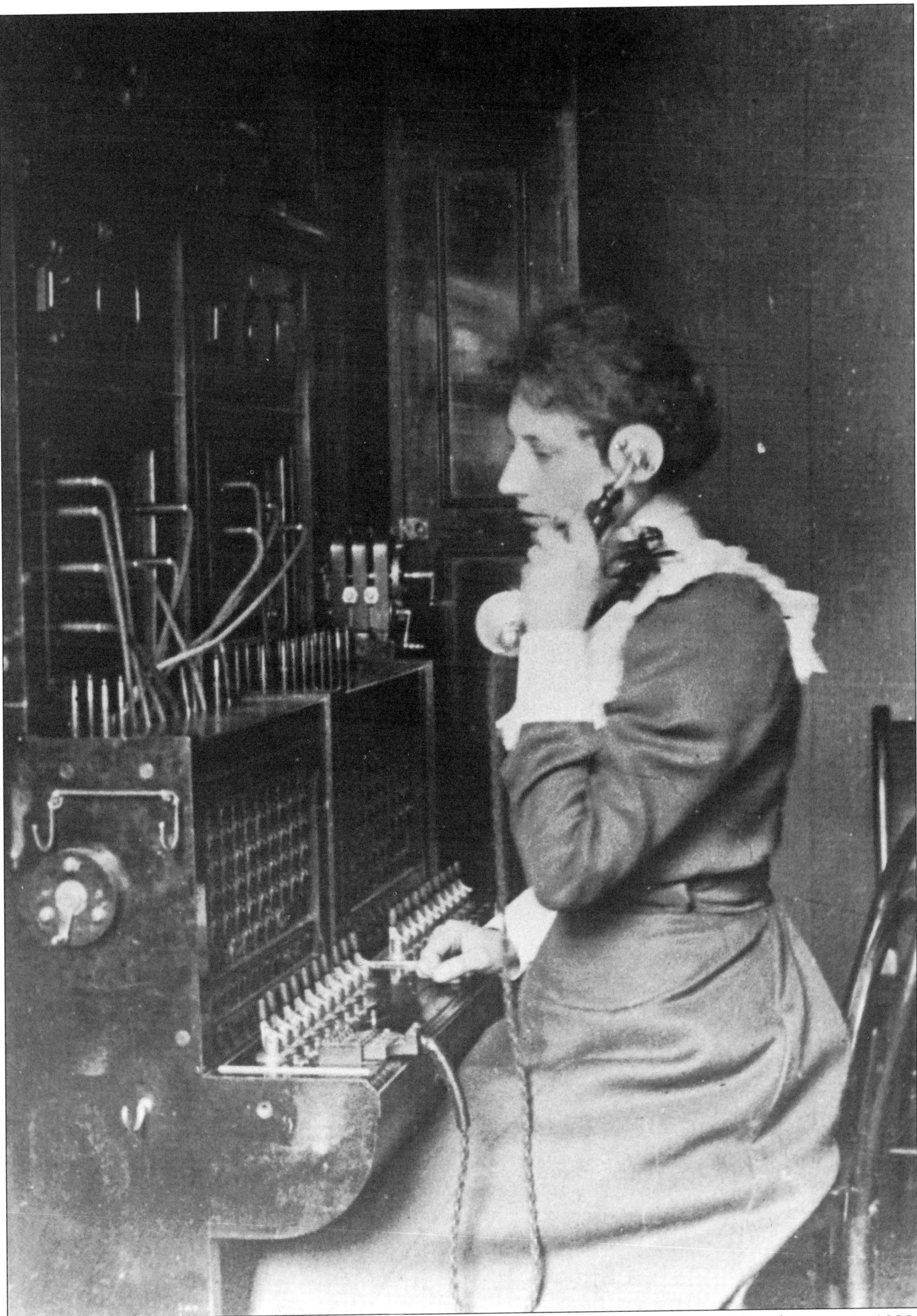

This is Miss Rushall, seen at the National Telephone Company's exchange in Little Church Street in 1898, soon after it was opened.

Time for repair at Rugby telephone exchange in the 1960s.

Operators at Rugby's computerised telephone exchange in 1989.

Railway Terrace slaughter-house in 1969.

Rugby at Play

Recreation has played a big part in the life of Rugby and this chapter shows part of it. It includes the Recreation Ground, some of the many cinemas which were dotted around the town, and even a line-up of lovelies in the Miss Rugby contest.

Small boys pose for the camera during a band contest on Rugby Recreation Ground on April 1, 1907.

The championship-winning athletics team of Elborow Boys' School in 1908.

A British tank on display at Rugby Recreation Ground, Whitehall Road, shortly after World War One. This is the path running parallel with Hillmorton Road.

The Rugby Town Silver Prize Band pictured in 1930 when they won the Daily Mirror Challenge Cup.

Removing the iron railings from Rugby Recreation Ground for the war effort in 1942.

The memorial gates at Rugby Recreation Ground in their prime, long before they were moved to make way for the road to the Ken Marriott Leisure Centre.

The memorial gates at Rugby Recreation Ground, Whitehall Road before they were moved just a few yards to make way for the controversial 'road through the rec'.

Lowering the memorial gates into their new resting place on June 7, 1987.

Autumn in Caldecott Park.

The Theatre Royal was built in Railway Terrace in October 1890, in Liddington's Field. This photograph was taken in 1899.

Walter Flavell was a well-known face in Rugby when he used to sell newspapers around the town. He lived in Railway Terrace and died about 35 years ago. Here he is advertising the Regent Cinema in Bank Street (*shown left*).

The Picture House in Bank Street opened in May 1920 and became the Regent Cinema in 1930. In 1936 it became the Regent Theatre and in July 1955 was re-named yet again, to The Century. It later closed and a Kwik Save supermarket took over the site.

The Rugby Palace Cinema in High Street, pictured before the building burned down on January 30, 1921. Vint's Palace Cinema on the site was first included in the *Rugby Directory* in 1913. After the fire the site was occupied by F.W.Woolworth.

The Regal Theatre, Railway Terrace, formerly the Prince of Wales Theatre, decorated for the coronation of King George VI in 1937.

The former cinema building in Henry Street became Rugby Theatre in 1949. It was previously the Empire Picture Palace and Scala Cinema.

The circus comes to town. Baby elephants are paraded along Regent Street in May 1970.

Digging foundations for the Ken Marriott Leisure Centre in the early 1970s.

The Ken Marriott Leisure Centre nearing completion in 1974. The photograph was taken from the field where the all-weather athletics track is now.

This photograph shows a mural painted in Chapel Street by local youth, as part of the 1982 Rugby Arts Festival.

Hopefuls line up for the 1973 Miss Rugby contest staged at the Benn Hall.

Barclay's Bank's winning float in the 1988 Rugby Carnival, based on the BBC TV *'Allo 'Allo* comedy programme.

The *Advertiser's* float in the 1989 carnival was based on *The Flintstones* TV cartoon series.

The Davina Bramley Dancing School's *Annie* float in 1989.

Rugby Theatre's *Peter Pan* pirate ship entry in the 1989 carnival.

Rugby *in* Rugby

One of Rugby's major claims to fame is being the birthplace of the game which bears its name. William Webb Ellis, a pupil at Rugby School, is credited with inventing the game on The Close in 1823. This chapter looks at some Rugby Football events in the town.

This is the earliest known team photograph of the Rugby Football Club, taken in 1878-79. The first reported match of the Rugby Crusaders (who became the Rugby Lions) was in December 1873.

Rugby RFC 2nd XV pictured in 1901-02. Standing (left to right): H.Greenfield, H.Willis, W.E.Bryan, G.H. Cave, J.W.L.Kennard, E.Franklin, W.Walton (touch judge). Seated: F.J.Smith, H.Colston, J.W.Bradford, J.R.Tait (captain), F.Hopkins, C.A.Taylor, J.E.Boyce. On ground: J.Fuller, F.Halliwell, W.H.Harris.

Following in the footsteps of William Webb Ellis, boys from Rugby School re-enact the original game for a film crew.

Rugby was honoured to host the launch of the Rugby World Cup on June 29, 1991. Here, Rugby Schoolboys re-enact the original game.

Rugby Lions celebrate victory against Newcastle Gosforth in April 1991, a victory which earned them the Second Division title and promotion to the top flight of the Courage League. The game was watched by 3,000 spectators at Webb Ellis Road and concluded their rise from Area League North to the First Division in four seasons.

All Blacks giant Jonah Lomu visited Rugby in November 1995. Hundreds of fans turned out to see New Zealand's 20-year-old hero of the Rugby World Cup.

Master craftsman John Batchelor demonstrates the making of rugby balls to pupils from Harris CE High School in the early 1980s. In January 1996 he was presented with a portrait to commemorate 40 years of work at the James Gilbert Rugby Football Museum. In that time he believes he has made more than 60,000 balls.

Village Life

Dunchurch, although only a short distance from Rugby, has maintained its independence from the town. This photograph shows Dunchurch Road in 1890. It is commonly known as 'Catholic Hill' because St Marie's Roman Catholic Church can be seen dominating the view. The rough gravel footpath and road were separated by a drainage channel.

In the early 1920s, the war memorial at Dunchurch was unveiled. Originally to honour those local men who had fallen in World War One it now includes names from both world wars.

Bilton Hall was built in the 17th century and is now divided into several homes. Bilton is now virtually part of Rugby but despite that it is very much its own community.

Bilton Green pictured in the early years of this century.

Another view of Bilton Green when life was played out at a much more tranquil pace.

Horse riders and a few pedestrians make up this scene of old Bilton.

Like Bilton, Clifton, on the other side of Rugby, also has its own special identity. This is Vicarage Hill after the road was widened in 1906 and the site of today's Butler's Leap.

The village pond at Clifton-on-Dunsmore at the turn of the century.

Newbold was once a very separate community from Rugby, but today it is virtually part of the town. This photograph shows a road in the village at the turn of the century.

The Avon Inn at Newbold in 1911. The decorations are presumably for the coronation of King George V.

Local children take part in the traditional May Day celebrations in Newbold in 1936.

This was how Parkfield Road, Newbold, looked in 1967 when flood water inundated the area.

Snapshots

A group of Boy Scouts from Rugby pose for the camera in 1910.

This May Day photograph was taken around 1920 and shows youngsters from Queen's Street and Russell Street in Rugby, dressed up for the occasion.

This photograph, taken in 1929, is of Rugby St John Ambulance cadets with Supt. Hazell and Chief Officer Harper.

Newbold St Botolph's Boy Scout group on parade in 1931.

All smiles at St Marie's School in 1932-33.

New Bilton St Oswald's Rugby Football Club pictured in the garden of the Holly Bush pub in season 1936-37.

In 1937 Rugby Rag Week attracted all kinds. These revellers are dressed for a fun time.

Members of Rugby's ambulance service pictured at the outbreak of World War Two.

This is 'J' Company of the Rugby Home Guard pictured during World War Two.

A touch of class. Sir Halford and Lady Reddish cut a cake to celebrate the issue of 'A' shares to employees of Rugby Portland Cement. It took place after the staff Christmas party when they staged a *Black and White Minstrel Show*.

The Rugby Federation of Anglers undertaking a fish rescue operation at Mr Dobson's pit in May 1969.

While the United States was celebrating Independence Day on July 4, 1980. Rugby was welcoming Prime Minister Margaret Thatcher when she went walkabout in the town centre.

This was the aftermath of a fire at the Old Red Lion pub in Harborough Magna in the summer of 1986.

The statue of Rugby's famous poet, Rupert Brooke, was unveiled by Dr Mary Archer in September 1988. She and her husband, Jeffrey Archer, live in Brooke's former house at Grantchester, Cambridge. The statue stands in Jubilee Gardens, Regent Place.

The Rugby Advertiser

The Word on the Street

The *Rugby Advertiser* is exactly 150 years old, having been launched in 1846. It is a weekly paid-for tabloid newspaper and the town's longest established newspaper. It is still the biggest selling. But the paper started life in March 1846 as the *Monthly Advertiser*, priced one old penny.

It was founded by William Ironside Tait, whose descendants still live in the town, and in fact it was his great great grandson, Richard Avery, who in March 1996 unveiled a plaque at the front of the building to commemorate the anniversary. The paper was bought by Heart of England Newspapers in the late 1960s and then by Emap Newspaper Division in the late 1980s and is produced by their Central Counties Newspapers Ltd publishing company, based in Aylesbury, Bucks.

The early years of the *Advertiser* saw little local news, although the paper had offices in Rugby, Nuneaton and Kineton. After World War Two the *Advertiser* introduced editions covering Lutterworth and Daventry.

The publication was printed in-house in Rugby until the late 1960s, when it moved initially to Nuneaton and later Leamington. Today the editorial part of the paper is produced totally in

Above, left: William Ironside Tait, who founded the *Rugby Advertiser* on March 7, 1846. He died on New Year's Eve 1875. *Above, right:* On February 6, 1897, the *Advertiser's* gas engine broke down and the UDC loaned their steam roller to drive the newspaper's printing machine. *Left:* One of the *Advertiser's* delivery vans pictured in 1926.

Rugby, including the scanning of colour and black and white pictures. The advertisements are typeset at Typestart, Kettering, and printed at Goodhead Press, Bicester.

A cornerstone of the town the *Rugby Advertiser* aims to be an essential part of the community, accurately reflecting events and activities of the people. Every week it is packed with news, views and sport for its readers.

The *Advertiser* has a sister publication, the *Rugby Review*, which is also published on a Thursday. The *Review* carries no editorial, but is the clear market leader for advertising.

The current editor of the *Advertiser* is Peter Aengenheister, who is only the thirteenth in the paper's history, and managing director of the Central Counties Newspapers Ltd, the parent publishing company, is Mr Ron Mitchell.

A corner of the news composing room showing the Monotype keyboard operators at work in the 1920s.

A general view of the newspaper's composing room, showing the Linotype.

The editor and managing director of 1926, Mr Sydney T.Watkins (seated) and former manager Mr E.E.Hopewell (left) with ex-editor Mr Frank Betts (right).

The *Rugby Advertiser* building in 1934, when the newspaper was written, typeset and printed on the same premises. These are still the *Advertiser* and *Rugby Review* offices, but typesetting and printing is now done elsewhere.

In the summer of 1959, a nationwide strike among printers in the regional newspaper industry saw many papers produce emergency editions. Here, Mr L.Stewart, Mr P.Fletcher and Gordon Tew use a hand-driven duplicating machine to keep *Advertiser* on the streets of Rugby.

Typesetting and printing was being done in the *Advertiser* buildings as late as 1966, when this was taken. Setting type was a very complex job and a worker can be seen here placing type-slugs into a galley.

Our Staff

This year, 1996, sees the *Rugby Advertiser* celebrating 150 years of news coverage, since its founder, William Ironside Tait, launched the paper in 1846.

In recognition of the current staff who perpetuate that work today, we would like to give special mention to these following people:

Editorial

Peter Aengenheister – Editor.
Gordon Birch – Assistant Editor (news).
Amanda Cotterill – Assistant Editor (production).
Zoe Ashton – Sports Editor.
Lucie Allen, Will Rankin and Jane Gould – Reporters.
Jemma Hall – Editorial Assistant.
Steve Cutner – Chief Photographer.
James Robbins and Anne-Marie Turner – Photographers.

Today's production techniques are a little more sophisticated. *Advertiser* editor, Peter Aengenheister scans a colour picture.

The *Advertiser* is always out getting people's views. Here, senior reporter Lucie Allen interviews a reader for the newspaper's vox pop feature 'The Word on the Street'.

Advertising
Michelle Roche – Advertisement Manager.
Classified: Karen Thomas and Ginny Johnson – team leaders; Marcia Sullivan, Maria Maltby, Joanne Perkins, Kelly Humphries and Rebecca Hogan.
Representatives: Tracey Schoales – display manager; Lindsey Ottley, Gail Dunkley and Tracy Hitchcox.

Reception
Sinead Phillips – Senior Receptionist; Ilona Roswell and Christine Falconer.

Accounts
Sylvia Wright.

Administrators
Margaret Mitchell and Angela Edwards.

Circulation
Liz Cunnington – Newspaper Sales Manager.

Circulation and promotions
Debbie Jarrold, Ann Mountford, Terri Short and Lisa Northrop.

The *Advertiser* is renowned for its friendliness and award-winners for caring for customers. Here senior receptionist Sinead Phillips greets a member of the public.

Below: Making sure that the papers reach the right people. Debbie Jarrold sets off for the newsagents.

Subscribers

The *Rugby Advertiser* and publishers Breedon Books would like to thank all the following preferential subscribers and hope they gain much enjoyment from their copy of *Images of Rugby.*

Shane Bryans
Nell Catlin
Mr D Cave
Beryl Claricoats
Mr Leonard Colling
Matthew David Crane
Osman G Evans
Alan Gammidge
Karl Gilbert
Denise Gill
Ruth Greer
Mr David Holton
Mark Howes
Wendy & Tony Howes
R John Hutchinson
Valerie Jaques
E D Jones
Mrs M W Keymer
A J King
Miss V Leeson
David Mead
Mrs Morris
Ronald H Overton
Patricia & Frank Preece
V Prowse
K G Richardson & P Hill, t/a Ross Hammond
Mrs G Sammon
William J Shipp
Elaine Smith
N Smith
Peggy Smith
Richard John Smith
V Stewart
Michael Taylor
David Tew
Dennis H Walden
Reginald S Walley
Anne & Jeff Way
Mrs Clare Webster
Mr M K Widnall
John Wrighton